Holistic Wellness Treatments
For
Total Wellbeing, Beauty, and
Health

Pamper Yourself to the Max from the Comfort of Your Home

By Marta Tuchowska

D1741046

www.holisticwellnessproject.com

Holistic Wellness Treatments

Disclaimer:

The author of this book is not a doctor and it is not her intention to claim that the treatments described in this book can be a substitute for professional medical advice or any standard medical treatments. Her aim is to simply present certain alternative and holistic therapies that can be applied at home. If you are suffering from any serious or chronic disease(s) or condition(s), or if you are on medication (even if natural, e.g. homeopathy), please consult with a medical or naturopathy doctor before you start using aromatherapy. Natural therapies are very safe to use, but please keep in mind the precautions that are included in this book. Not all the aromatherapy treatments are safe for women who are pregnant, so please consult with your doctor and/or aromatherapist first. Always check the safety information supplied with any new oil, research the brand, and make sure that the products you buy for your home spa are 100% natural and organic.

Introduction Holistic Wellness Spa Temptation

I want to thank you for purchasing the book: *Holistic Wellness Treatments*. If you are passionate about Wellness, Relaxation and Natural Therapies, then you will love this book. You will discover many simple, inexpensive and effective ways to create your home spa to de-stress and revitalize in a very inexpensive way.

If you have read the first part of *Holistic Wellness Spa series: Aromatherapy and Essential Oils for Beginners* and wish to learn more about aromatherapy and other natural spa treatments, this book will offer you many more advanced techniques and ideas. If you haven't read it yet, don't worry: this book also summarizes the most important aromatherapy rules that you need to get started.

Hippocrates, the father of medicine, strongly advocated the use of therapeutic plants and herbs as well as their healing essences. According to his teachings, to enjoy a strong and healthy life one should bathe in aromatic waters regularly and treat oneself to a daily massage with scented oils. Today, with the popularity of spas and spa treatments, aromatherapy massage is well recognized and widely practiced. You can easily access the whole range of highly personalized aromatherapy treatments and other natural therapies inexpensively from the comfort of your own home. Creating your own spa treatments at home is the fun part, and your imagination alone sets the limits of what you can do.

Apart from relaxation and beauty treatments, you will also learn how to create your home health spa with a Bonus Chapter on Body & Mind Detoxifying Diet Weekend Program (Chapter 6). I have tried my best to make it as holistic as possible.

Take a few deep breaths, relax, put on some relaxing music and read on!

Chapter 1 Aromatherapy as a Holistic Therapy

Holistic Therapies are also known as 'alternative therapies' or 'alternative medicine', and they are based on the belief that the human body can heal itself if given the proper stimulants. For example, it can be a natural therapy like homeopathy, herbs or body work, such as shiatsu, massage or acupuncture. The oriental branches of medicine, e.g. Ayurveda or Chinese medicine, are considered to be holistic therapies. The word 'holistic' comes from Latin and means 'the entire; whole', and all natural therapies underline the connection between the body, mind, spirit and emotions. Holistic Therapies also stress the importance of disease prevention and make healthy, balanced living a priority.

How many times have you come down with the flu or another infection after a stressful period of your life or after experiencing some stress in the workplace? You have probably noticed that avoiding or fighting stress results in better health and when you feel better in your body, you also feel emotionally stronger and can focus more easily. If, on the other hand, something goes wrong and you go through a tough patch, you start accumulating pain, negativity and very often disease. I am sure that you have already noticed this connection by simply observing your body, your thoughts, and your emotions.

Oriental medicine is based on a belief that one is responsible for one's own health, and that the art of learning a stress-free life and taking care of oneself in a fully holistic way should be priorities. Unfortunately, our Western, fast-paced society underlines the importance of goals that are mostly associated with financial success, and very often we get so success-driven that we forget about health. Consequently, over the years we start acquiring some serious stress-related medical conditions.

It is time to slow down and relax with aromatherapy. While aromatherapy oils can't be seen as a panacea for all the ailments, they offer a wide range of very pleasurable treatments that restore balance that the body and mind need to stimulate the process of healing. Aromatherapy is a holistic therapy as it is not only used for body treatments (e.g. beauty treatments or sore muscles), but it can also help people remain focused, overcome frustration, alleviate insomnia and anxiety, and bring overall peace of mind.

What is Aromatherapy and how does it work?

Aromatherapy is an art and science of blending and applying aromatic oils that are extracted from plants, trees, leaves and flowers. The aromatic oils are called essential oils, but they are not greasy at all. The consistency is similar to water or alcohol and they are filled with many naturally therapeutic active ingredients. Essential oils are very potent, so they can't be applied directly on to the skin because they may cause an allergic reaction. That is why it is necessary to blend them with a suitable cold-pressed vegetable oil, also called ''a carrier oil'' or ''a base oil'', such as for example avocado, olive-oil, or apricot.

There are various ways of employing aromatherapy, and there is even a branch of aromatherapy called 'phytoaromatherapy', or 'scientific aromatherapy', that advocates the internal use of the oils. The SPA, though, uses aromatherapy treatments mainly in two ways:

1. Aromatherapy Massage

2. Aromatherapy Bath and Inhalation.

The treatments described in this book follow mostly the British School of Aromatherapy, which underlines the importance of employing aromatherapy only topically, i.e. via massage or in an aromatic bath, and recommends using essential oils only when diluted in carrier oils in 2-5% concentrations. It excludes the use of undiluted essential oils or taken orally.

The British School encourages aromatherapy for massage and relaxation, as well as a means of dealing with some problems of an emotional nature, such as stress. This is why it has been widely adopted in a many spas and wellness resorts.There is also another approach called the French School of Aromatherapy, which is also called 'scientific aromatherapy' or 'aromatology'. It is much more complex and is very often employed by naturopathic doctors. This school stresses the importance of using chymotyped oils (e.g. rosemary oil can have two or more chemotypes, so the properties may slightly change) and advocates the internal use of essential oils as well as the use of them topically in undiluted form. This branch is very similar to herbalism. In order to employ a safe and effective treatment, it is always advisable to consult with a local aromatherapist or naturopathy doctor that specializes in oral aromatherapy treatments. It is also necessary to research the brand and make sure that the oils are organic and chymotyped.

The French School approach won't be included in this book as it is not normally practiced at spas. If you are interested in learning more about the French School of Aromatherapy, you can check resources such as *Chymotyped Essential Oils* by A.Zhiri, D.Baudoux, M.L. Breda.

Sympathetic System and Parasympathetic System

You can certainly distinguish between two emotional states. One of them is feeling good, happy, and stress-free. In this one, we experience moments of pleasure. There is also another state that none of us want to experience, yet very often we just fall its victim unwillingly. This state is feeling stressed, worried, unhappy, irritated, in pain and basically ready to indulge in our basic instinct: fight or flight. Whenever experiencing the first, more desirable state of being, you can say 'thank you' to the parasympathetic system that is responsible for experiencing all the sensations that we tag as pleasurable. The sympathetic system, on the other hand, is responsible for the body's reactions to stress, so whenever you feel nervous or are shaking and sweating, you can blame the sympathetic system of the brain.

Aromatherapy and gentle aromatherapy massage have two basic tasks: to stimulate the parasympathetic system and to relax the sympathetic system at the same time. Your body will have no choice but to finally relax.

Aromatherapy Massage

Massage brings immediate relief to muscle tension and is a great mood enhancer. Aromatherapy blends added to a massage increase its therapeutic properties. Aromatherapy massage is a great union of a natural therapy and a manual therapy that bring amazing results. Everyone loves getting pampered at spas, and aromatherapy massage is one of the treatments that are always in big demand. Unfortunately, many spa treatments are quite expensive, so following Hippocrates' teachings to have a daily aromatherapy massage can be all but impossible to afford. Luckily, you can treat yourself to a daily self- massage with your own, personalized aromatherapy blends, and adjust it according to your mood and how you feel. Aromatherapy will work exactly the same as it would if it was applied from the hands of an experienced masseuse: the oils get absorbed by the skin and get into the circulatory system where their therapeutic properties start to do their job. If one seeks professional massage therapy, it can only be found from the hands of an experienced therapist, but using aromatherapy massage at home for aromatherapy purposes only is as simple as using a body lotion (though aromatherapy oils bring more benefits).

Apart from a physical effect that causes chemical changes in your body's systems (the endocrine system, the lymphatic system, the circulatory system, and the nervous system), there is also an immediate psychological effect when you inhale the fragrance. To enhance it further, remember to breathe in deeply and enjoy the aromatic moments as much as you can. To gain the maximum benefit from an aromatherapy massage, do not shower or bathe for 8 hours after the massage and drink plenty of water to flush away toxins.

Aromatherapy General Precautions

Aromatherapy is a very safe and easy therapy to use, but keep in mind that there are certain precautions:

- Remember to wash your hands after applying aromatherapy massage;

- Do not apply the essential oils in their pure form as they may cause an allergic reaction. Instead, use blends that contain 2-5% essential oils diluted in good-quality cold-pressed oil;

- Do not apply oils after surgery (unless you have consulted with a doctor) or on open wounds or rashes of unknown origin;

- Do not use the oils after chemotherapy (unless suggested by a doctor);

- Keep the oils away from the eyes and mucus membranes;

- Use the oils only topically (unless you have consulted with an aromatherapist who specializes in phytoaromatherapy);

- Avoid rosemary, thyme, Spanish and common sage, fennel and hyssop if you suffer from high blood pressure;

- Do not apply the treatments described in this book on babies or infants. It doesn't mean that aromatherapy can never be used on babies and infants, but extremely low concentrations should be used. Always consult with a medical or naturopathy doctor first;

- After an aromatherapy massage always remember to wash your hands;

- Make sure that you research the brand, read safety instructions for each individual oil you buy/use and check the expiration date;

- Store your blends in dark glass bottles, preferably in a cool, dry and dark place and remember to use within a maximum of one month after mixing.

Aromatherapy Blends/Rules

The basic rules to keep in mind are the following proportions:

-For 15ml of vegetable oil (table spoon) add 5- 7 drops of essential oil.

-For 2ml of vegetable oil add 1 drop of essential oil.

If you are working on the face, use weaker concentrations, especially if you have sensitive skin:

For 30ml of a vegetable oil (or cream) use 1- 2 drops of essential oil.

If you wish to perform a facial treatment with aromatherapy oil, first apply the blend to the wrists to ensure that there is no allergic reaction. Avoid using oils like clove, cinnamon, oregano, rosemary and thyme if you have a sensitive skin that goes red easily.

There are many vegetable oils that you can use as carrier oils for your blends: sweet almond oil, grape seed oil, hazelnut oil, olive oil, and avocado oil are the most popular for massage.

Chapter 2 The Power of Natural Beauty Treatments

How do you normally feel after long hours of computer work or when you get a headache? You probably intuitively rub your temples, touch your neck or ask someone to press your shoulders. The feeling of relaxation brings immediate relief. What if you could actually combine beauty treatments with body and mind relaxation? Wouldn't it be also a great way to safe some time, too?

Unfortunately, most of us Westerners limit beauty treatments to a simple cosmetic routine and look for relaxation elsewhere. In the first part of my book I mentioned that the standard chemical beauty products and beauty treatments may be able to mask the problem in the short-term, but that they offer no benefits for the mind and can be detrimental to one's health and the environment in the long run. There is a big seller's market for all kinds of products like anti-wrinkle creams that claim to make you look ten years younger, and those companies make tons of money. The approach that I suggest is less expensive and much more holistic.

To begin with:

- Have a look at your diet. Reduce the amount of toxins (smoking, drinking, processed foods), add more fresh and organically grown fruits and vegetables, and drink plenty of water.

- Try to get away from the city at least once a week and disconnect your mobile devices.

- Do more exercise whenever you can. Walk or cycle instead of driving when possible.

- Try to perform a regular face massage using natural oils according to your skin type.

Let me focus on my last suggestion as this is the main point of this chapter: the benefits of facial massage are very often overlooked and many people think that it is a procedure that is strictly restricted to women. Of course, we ladies tend to take care more of our skin than men, but regular facial massage is a great natural treatment for everyone.

What does facial massage do for those who employ them?

- Fights and prevents migraines and headaches;

- Enhances a person's mood;

- Helps alleviate insomnia and anxiety;

- Can help fight off colds and bring immediate relief for sinusitis victims.

- Increases focus and concentration.

You have probably realized that very often our emotional and physical strains are reflected in our facials expressions. It is not only about wrinkles, though. Certain uncontrolled emotional states that show themselves on the face turn into chronic tension that may result in migraines and headaches. The frontalis muscle that covers the forehead can easily accumulate stress and emotional tension. The muscle gets tense, and then spread the tension and pain on to the temporalis muscle (temple area). This can result in a bad migraine and low energy levels.

I hope that now you feel intrigued and ready to get started on your facial massage routine. The procedure is very easy and you will learn all about it in the next chapter. If you tend to suffer from migraines, whenever you feel that a headache is starting to kick in, massage your forehead energetically and then move to the temples area. Remember to always wash your face before a facial massage. It collects grime from the environment, makeup, and physical activity during the day. This grime should be removed with a gentle, natural cleaner.

You can prepare many natural skin tonics using herbal infusions, e.g. rosemary infusion, green tea, chamomile, mint, aloe vera juice, and mineral water with a few drops of lemon juice. You can prepare your favorite infusion to drink and at the same time use a certain amount to refresh your skin. In order to remove makeup, try natural vegetable oils, such as grape seed oil or sweet almond oil. This will give you a great natural alternative to chemical makeup removers and lotions that may be occupying way too much space in your bathroom cupboard. Moreover, you can use vegetable oils as a body lotion, hair conditioner and body massage as well as for aromatherapy blends.

Your skin will really appreciate it if you give it a break and switch to natural solutions. Healthy skin that looks great doesn't require wearing a lot of heavy makeup. I am not saying that you can't use makeup, but it feels great to have the freedom to use it more as an occasional choice rather than a necessity. Naturally healthy and radiant skin is definitely a sign of overall health and vitality. It may take more work to achieve it, but it is definitely worth it.

Chapter 3 Holistic Beauty Treatments

Before you get started on a facial self-massage it is important that you know your skin type, as this knowledge will help you to select the proper oils and personalize the treatment. Most women probably know their skin type and know which category they fall into, but for men it can be a tricky task. Very often our skin is also prone to hormonal changes that occur with age, so it is important to take more care of it as we get older.

Let's have a look at different skin types:

- **Oily Skin** is very common in teenagers and at menstruation. It is advisable for those with oily skin to drink lots of water and fresh, organic juices and reduce over consumption of sugar and salt so as not to stimulate the sebaceous glands.

The essential oils recommended for oily skins are: verbena, palmarosa, bergamot, lavender, and geranium, which adapts to different skin types and can also be used for dry or mixed skin.

You can add them to a natural cream or a natural face mask as well as aloe vera gel, which has a light consistency but is also extremely hydrating. Occasionally, you can also use vegetable oils to dilute the essential oils. Though many beauticians would object to it, the oily skin actually needs to get properly hydrated and a weekly massage with oils such as evening primrose oil or grape seed oil enriched by the above mentioned essential oils can regulate sebum secretion.

Natural ingredients used for oily skin masks include: cucumber, lemon, oats, green clay, strawberries, bananas and apples. You can create your own masks choosing your favorite ingredients and adding your favorite essential oils to make them more personalized.

- **Dry Skin** - Dry skin is normally prone to premature aging, so it must be treated with natural oils and creams that moisturize it. A person with dry skin should also drink plenty of water and avoid caffeine. Many women who go through menopause, pregnancy or menstruation suffer from dry skin, and men who undergo hormonal changes may experience drying up of the skin as well. Certain conditions like eczema, psoriasis and dermatitis can be blamed on extremely dry skin as well.

Essential oils for dry skin include: ylang-ylang, Peru balsam, German and Roma chamomile and palmarosa. You should use some highly hydrating natural creams or oils as a base: argan oil, coconut oil, sweet almond oil, avocado oil or apricot kennels are really good choices. Shea butter and jojoba oil (or jojoba wax) will also help re-hydrate.

- **Mature Skin** -Mature skin tends to lose moisture more rapidly, so it should be treated with the same care as dry skin. When doing a facial massage it is generally recommended not to use too much pressure and to work within its limit of slightly reduced elasticity. Mature skin is normally thinner and has more wrinkles, which some people worry about, whereas it should be perceived more as a valuable richness of life experience and wisdom.

You can use jasmine, sweet fennel and rosewood essential oils. You may want to substitute your night cream for vegetable oils enriched with essential oils with hydrating properties. Moroccan argan oil is said to maintain an eternal youth, and many natural products for mature skin include it as a main ingredient. Argan oil is also a great natural hair conditioner. Other vegetable oils recommended are castor oil and jojoba oil.

- **Sensitive Skin** - This type of skin reddens easily when touched and when treated with many too many creams and lotions. Sometimes it can take years to find the proper care for sensitive skin, and each case can be different. The safest essential oils to use include German and Roman chamomile diluted in a natural, gentle cream or vegetable oils such as avocado oil or argan oil (some skins may redden though). Aloe vera gel or cream is also a good base to dilute your chosen essential oils.

- **Combination Skin** - Taking proper care of this type of skin can be more time consuming if you want to do it in a natural way because it is a combination of dry, oily and even sensitive, along with normal skin type. The 'T' zone (forehead, nose and chin) tends to be the oily area. Some areas, normally the cheeks, can be very sensitive. You can use essential oils like geranium or palmarosa as they tend to adapt to different skin types and regulate sebum secretion. As a base, use a natural cream or aloe vera gel, and if you need to hydrate the oily parts, use vegetable oils instead. Treat the oily areas with a green clay mask twice a week and make sure you always remove your makeup and clean your skin with natural, organic products.

I hope that following my general guidelines will give you some ideas and inspiration for some blends that you can prepare for your facial massage. The technique described will work not only for your skin but also for your mind, stimulating relaxation and eliminating stress. This is why it can be described as a Holistic Beauty Treatment. I hope that you will enjoy this ritual!

Facial massage precautions:

Avoid working on areas that are affected by eczema, conjunctivitis, abscess and boils, cold sores, impetigo, and/or warts.

Facial massage is totally contraindicated for people suffering from skin cancer.

Simple steps to perform a holistic facial massage (or: self-massage)

- The techniques suggested come from Swedish Massage, Neurosedative Massage and Indian Face Massage.

1. Mix the oils and apply small amounts at a time. Gently stroke the face with the pads of your fingertips. Do it slowly but try to maintain a steady rhythm. This gentle stroke is called

neurosedative touch and it stimulates relaxation. Breathe in deeply, hold it for a few seconds, and then breathe out slowly.

2. If needed, apply some more oils to make sure that the skin is moist enough to do a massage, but avoid over-applying oils as your hands would then be losing contact with the skin. If the area gets too slippery, it's harder to do the treatment.

3. Using the area of the hand just below the thumb (the mound at the base) try moving your hand in circles around on the forehead. This technique will eliminate accumulated tension. Work on the forehead and then move to the temples, cheeks and chin area. The jaws can also accumulate great amounts of tension. If you feel any knots or tension, work the affected area a bit longer. Follow your intuition also as it tends to be much more effective than following massage protocols (which are good for getting started). Repeat a few times, doing one side at a time: work on the left, then the right side of the face. Keep switching. You may notice that one side of the face has more accumulated tension than the other. This is normal.

4. Using your fingers of both hands, gently make circles on the skin around the forehead, then move to the temples area and down to the jaw and chin area.

5. Using the pads of your fingers, gently squeeze the eyebrows and keep increasing the pressure. This technique is best performed employing your middle fingers and the thumbs. It also brings a great relief to a frontalis muscle and prevents migraines and headaches.

6. Using all your fingers - the pads of your thumbs plus the pads of the rest of the fingers - gently squeeze the chin and then move up to the jaws area. You may also want to experiment with moving your jaw to release tension.

7. Pressure points - For this technique, you will be using the pads of your thumbs (or middle/index fingers, whichever works best for you) pressing different points on your face to enhance the therapeutic and healing effect of the massage.

Ayurvedic Massage and Shiatsu and Chinese Acupressure are all disciplines that work with these powerful points to stimulate healing. I only present an extremely simplified review of some of the oriental manual therapies, but you will be amazed at the results!

Each point should be worked on for about 10-15 seconds and then released, and the whole procedure can be repeated again on the same point. Focus on the points that bring an immediate relief to you or your recipient as well as points that accumulate pain or tension. (This is a sign of some inner imbalance that can be healed with manual therapy.)

- Apply gentle but firm pressure to the middle of the forehead between the eyebrows. This point is called the Third Eye in Ayurvedic Medicine. *Then* work the eyebrows, simply applying the pressure on the points following the eyebrows line and stopping on the point where the eyebrows finish. Press it using the same technique and then work the temple areas. Applying pressure there can bring relief if you suffer from sinusitis.

- From the temples, start moving up following the hairline. According to Chinese acupressure, working on the hairline is an inseparable part of a face or head massage as it brings focus, concentration and calms nerves at the same time.

When your two hands meet in the centre of the hairline, you can also apply the pressure to your scalp following the middle line. Get back to the hairline using the same path and move down to the *third eye* again and apply pressure.

- After working the *third eye*, apply pressure under the eyes in line with the pupils and hold for 10- 15 seconds. From there, move your hands down and work the corners of the mouth. There are pressure points approximately 1 inch away from the corners of the mouth.

- Gently rub the earlobes.

Going through the steps described above will bring feelings of relaxation and focus. Moreover, you can always skip the oils part and simply do the pressure points part, which is a great solution if you are at work or have limited time.

If you do it on someone else, they will almost certainly ask you to do it again!

Chapter 4 Mindfulness Exercises

This chapter will teach you some basic relaxation techniques that, when blended with aromatherapy and the tranquility of your home spa, will result in the ultimate wellness experience. The exercises described are a combination of relaxation techniques and reiki and are based on the concept of mindfulness and subtle energy. How many times have you felt that someone was looking at you even though you had your back turned to them? You could intuitively feel that they were staring at you. Why do you feel good in certain environments whereas at the same time the appearance of certain individuals may simply spoil the atmosphere and bring in some 'bad' energy?

Some people are more sensitive than others, and so is their intuition. Regular meditation or relaxation in a mindful way can increase one's intuition and awareness. If performed on a regular basis and mastered, it can also bring many other benefits, such as detoxifying the system, helping the individual to gain more intuition and focus, controlling the person's emotions, and stimulating the immune system.

The following relaxation techniques can be safely practiced by anyone to increase mindfulness:

- Hold your hands out in front of you. Your palms should be facing each other but not touching at all. Allow your hands to close very slowly. Concentrate on your breath. Breathe in deeply and breathe out slowly. Choose your own rhythm and bring all your attention to your hands, let them move away and bring them back close, but make sure that they are not touching each other. After several repetitions you may start experiencing the sensation of warmth between your hands and this sensation may be spreading on to your body. This is what many therapists and reiki practitioners call *healing energy*. If you don't feel anything, don't worry about it but focus on your breathing and imagine a big ball of energy, like the Sun, between your hands.

- Slowly move the ball of energy up and place it on your head. Put your hands on your head, relax, keep breathing and imagine the cascading energies of light that enter your body through your head and spread into all directions. You may want to concentrate on the areas that are in pain, or even on certain emotions that need healing.

- Finally stroke your face, arms, legs and the whole body, and to finish, shake your hands off, imagining the dust that is leaving your body so that the healing can occur.

Another technique consists of using all your senses to imagine that you are a tree:

-Take in a deep breath and close your eyes, slowly exhale and relax.

- Imagine that your feet are in soil or compost or the warm sand on a beach. Use all your senses to actually feel it.

- Imagine that your toes are roots and they are going deeper and deeper into the soil. This technique is you grounding yourself and is very often used by massage and holistic therapists so that they can enhance their focus and work effectively

- Take your time and don't rush it. With your hands in the prayer position, or a reverent position that feels right to you, close your eyes and take a deep breath.

-Exhale slowly and imagine that a bright white light is entering you from the top of your head. Feel, sense or see the light flowing through your body. You may feel a sense of calmness and relaxation now. If so, just allows it to happen. Take your time doing these exercises. There is no need to rush it. Just relax and enjoy the feelings going through you.

If you are intrigued by these exercises and would like to learn more, I recommend that you do reiki initiation with a local reiki master, as this will give you some extremely powerful tools to develop more relaxation techniques to increase wellbeing and healing.

If you feel sceptical about the exercise I described, you may wish to try this simple five senses meditation:

- Sit comfortably and breathe in deeply. When you are ready, try to evoke a place or an image from your childhood that you really loved and that brings positive memories and associations. I will give you an example of how I do it so that you can adjust it and make it work for you:

- I imagine a kitchen at my grandma's place. First of all, I focus on the colors and all the visual sensations, anything that I can remember. I just scan the walls, the drawers, the cooker, even the calendar on the wall. I then go to the window and have a look at the city. I can see the sky, the trees, the cars, the people, the trams, and even the snow on the sidewalk. I take my time to enjoy the view.

- I then start smelling the dinner and the wonderful cake and other fragrances that I associate with being taken care of and stress-free. I open the fridge and all the cupboards and take different foods and items from there and smell them: the coffee, the herbs, the spices. I take all the fruits and smell them.

- Then I focus on the sounds around me: the sounds from the streets, my grandma and my grandpa talking, the TV, the boiling water, even the birds singing.

- I then start tasting the delicious pancakes that my grandma prepared for me. I eat them slowly and analyse the taste of each and every ingredient. I taste the juice and other things that were prepared especially for me.

- Now it's time to experience the sensation of touch...I go to the bedroom and decide to have a nap. I fall on the bed and can feel the softness of the mattress, the cushions and the blanket. I keep breathing and relaxing. Finally, I close my eyes and focus on the wonderful smell of lavanda.

Try this go-back-in-time technique and use all of your senses to experience a magical sense of relaxation and well being. I found it very interesting that most of the people choose to go back to their childhood and very often they also choose their grandparent's place, which was the best spa ever when we were kids!

I have a guided meditation that you can download for free at:

www.holisticwellnessproject.com/meditation

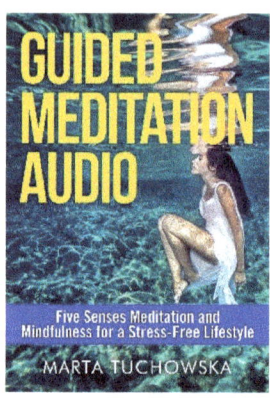

Chapter 5 Rejuvenate Your Body, Mind, & Spirit

Now that you know how to relax and how to blend the oils, it is time to get to know some essential oils that will open the door to the whole range of treatments for you. There are hundreds of them, and aromatherapy is a life-long study. The world of essential oils offers endless blends, not only to soothe and calm the nerves, but also to alleviate many physical, mental and emotional stress-related complaints. Essential oils are an intrinsic part of holistic beauty treatments.

When purchasing the oils, make sure that they are organic, and get acquainted with the possible precautions that the oils' providers list on the products. Unfortunately, there are many aromatherapy suppliers who are more concerned about their own profit than the quality of their products. Consulting a local aromatherapist should help you choose the right brand. Another option is visiting health food shops, as they normally sell high quality brands. I have already listed the main precautions in Chapter 1, but I would also like you to remember that:

- All the essential oils must be diluted in vegetable base oils before being applied to the skin

There are many vegetable oils that you can use, including sweet almond oil, avocado oil, and olive oil, and you can also use natural creams or lotions and aloe vera gel.

- Avoid applying to skin on top of other skincare products.

- Check out the expiration date before using.

- Do not use near an open flame.

- Do not use too many essential oils in one blend. 1- 3(max.5 in some cases) essential oils per blend is enough.

- Store blends in a cool, dark, dry place. Be careful about using kitchen cupboards (steam and heat from cooking may affect their potency), the fridge (too cold), and the bathroom cupboard (can get too hot and steamy).

I store all my essential oils in a wooden box in a bedroom wardrobe.

The following list of some of my favorite essential oils will help you create highly personalized blends for you and your loved ones. In the first part of Create Your Holistic Wellness Spa at Home I listed some popular essential oils, such as rosemary, lavender and bergamot. In this chapter I mention some oils with which you may be unfamiliar.

While the descriptions of some oils may sound tempting or like something that your body and mind may need, **a more intuitive approach** is to smell the oils and choose the fragrance that you like most. Normally we are attracted to oils that produce results that are to us, and very often intuition can be more helpful than scientific information. I hope that you become interested in trying at least a few oils from the list below. How can you get started?

1. First, analyze the reason for the treatment. Then choose the oils that are recommended for those who have your problem and prepare your own blend. Then apply it and to see how it works for you.

2. Depending on which treatment you wish to perform, choose one of the following ways to apply your blend:

- Physical tension or beauty treatments - Massage the areas affected. For example, if you suffer from sore muscles, choose the oils that work best, mix them and massage them in. If you wish to reduce cellulite, prepare your blend of oils and apply twice a day.

- Stress, problems of an emotional nature, insomnia or anxiety
- Choose your favorite soothing oils and perform a full-body

massage, or treat yourself to an aromatherapy bath. Panic attacks, nervousness, frustration, anger and anxiety situations can be alleviated by massaging the solar plexus and the feet.

- Skin problems - Add one drop of your chosen essential oil to your cream or face mask. If you have sensitive skin, test on your wrists first to avoid an allergic reaction.

- Headaches, including migraines - Use the blend to massage your neck, shoulders, head and temples. Avoid contact with the eyes.

- To improve your hair condition - perform a scalp massage and leave in the oils for at least 1 hour. Then wash your hair in a gentle shampoo. For damaged or brittle hair leave it in overnight.

- Common cold - Use your blends to massage the neck, temples (be careful about the eye area), chest, and back. You can also massage your feet.

- Indigestion or menstrual pains - Gently massage your stomach and lower back. Remember that aromatherapy massage can alleviate the occasional digestion problem, but if your condition persists, consult with a medical doctor.

- To unwind - Prepare an aromatherapy relaxing bath. Add your aromatherapy blend only when the water is not running. Focus on your breathing and try to disconnect.

I have invited some very powerful essential oils that will introduce themselves and hopefully get invited to your home spa to work hard for your body & mind WELLNESS:

Essential Oils for your Home Spa

Picea Mariana-Black Spruce Essential Oil says:

Hi, my name is Black Spruce Essential Oil. The plant I am made of is native to Canada, and my mission is to eliminate muscular pain and to cheer you up as well! I smell delicious and would be very happy if you could include me in your blends.

For the Body:

- It is great in blends for sinusitis and colds, acne, sore muscles, rheumatic pains, physical fatigue, and tension.

For the Mind & Emotions:

- It is a great mood stabilizer, and it can be both uplifting and sedating. Moreover, it is said to have some deep spiritual properties. It stimulates the process of grounding. If you are studying or doing any kind if mental activity and need more focus and inspiration, then Black Spruce is the oil for you. It also removes energy blockages, which results in an emotional peace.

Satureja Montana- Savory Essential Oil says:

Hi, my name is Savory Essential Oil and I am here to motivate you and energize you with my Sharp, herbaceous aroma!

For the Body:

- It stimulates the immune system and gives physical vitality.

- It is used to alleviate arthritis, rheumatic pains and back problems.

- It is used to treat: acne, athlete's foot and boil blends.

For the Mind & Emotions:

- It helps overcome disappointment.

- It encourages the feeling of unconditional love.

- It fights feelings of frustration.

Melaleuca Alternifolia- Tea Tree Oil says:

Hi, my name is Teatree Oil and my scent will make you feel like you are in the middle of the forest!

For the Body:

- It has some really strong antibacterial properties and is used to treat acne, spots, dandruff, oily skin, and oily scalp.

- It helps alleviate and prevent colds, coughs and sinusitis.

- It stimulates the lymphatic system and helps get rid of edemas. It also reduces water retention.

For the Mind & Emotions:

- It helps heal emotional wounds.

- It purifies the mind from unpleasant thoughts.

Melaleuca Cajuputii- Cajuput Essential Oil says:

Hi, my name is Cajuput Essential Oil and my mother plant is native to Australia. If you loved the smell of Tee Tree Oil then you will love mine as well. We both blend well together and are a perfect team to uplift your body & mind!

For the Body:

- Dandruff, oily scalp, pimples, herpes

- Colds, sinusitis and flu

For the Mind:

- Increases the feeling of here and now

- Improves concentration, but also relaxes and soothes

Coriandrum Sativum- Coriander Essential Oil says:

Hi, my name is Coriander Essential Oil and you might have heard of me because my mother plant is very famous in Indian cuisine. If you suffer from insomnia, I can definitely help you achieve deep, rejuvenating sleep. I also have many other properties!

For the Body:

- Helps treat arthritis, colds, flu, migraine, muscular aches, nausea, neuralgia, rheumatism, skin (oily), muscle stiffness.

For the Mind & Emotions:

- Helps overcome addictions and overeating

- Helps achieve deep relaxation and prevents excessive worrying

Cupressus Sempervirens var. Stricta- Cypress Leaf Provence Essential Oil says:

Hi, my name is Cypress Leaf Provence Essential Oil. My mother plant is native to Asia and I am here to relax your nervous system with my fresh scent. I have many properties, so make sure you include me in your blends:

For the Body:

- Reduces cellulite, edema, water retention

- Mitigates toxin accumulation

- Treats coughs and colds

For the Mind and Emotions:

- Alleviates anger and hurt feelings

- Helps with insomnia and anxiety

Artemisia Dracunculus- Tarragon Essential Oil says:

Hi, my name is Tarragon Essential Oil. My mother plant has some very strong antioxidant properties, and I am here to increase your energy levels and protect you from illnesses. Check my properties and include me in your blends!

For the Body:

- Reduces physical fatigue

- Mitigates toxin accumulation

- Treats nausea and headaches

- Alleviates muscular pain

- Sooths menstrual cramps

- Improves digestion

For the Mind & Emotions:

- Helps people move on with personal and professional changes

- Helps people recover emotionally after crises and other difficult situations

Gaultheria Procumbens- Wintergreen Essential Oil says:

Hi, my name is Wintergreen Essential Oil and I am also called a natural painkiller. You can use me for a range of blends for your body & mind:

For the Body:

- Natural anti-inflammatory properties can bring relief for sore muscles, backache, arthritis, colds, headaches, edema, carpal tunnel, fibromyalgia, sprains, varicose veins and inflammation

For the Mind & Emotions:

- Increases intuition

- Great for meditation

Cedrelopsis Grevei- Katrafay Essential Oil says:

Hi, my name is Katrafay Essential Oil and my mother plant is native to Madagascar. Just like Wintergreen Essential Oil, I am a natural painkiller because of my anti-inflammatory properties. I hope to get invited to your home Spa, too!

For the Body:

- Reduces cellulite and strae

- Alleviates rheumatic pains, tendinitis, arthritis

- Treats edema, varicose veins, slow circulation

- Soothes migraines and headaches

For the Mind & Emotions:

- Soothes chaotic mind

- Helps fight insomnia

- Helps people accept the truth and move forward

Citrus Sinesis- Sweet Orange Essential Oil says:

Hi, my name is Sweet Orange Essential Oil and my sweet, citric aroma will give you all the energy you need while relaxing you at the same time. Does it seem too contradictory? Include me in your blends and find out for yourself.

For the Body:

- Eases digestive problems

- Helps boost the lymphatic system and immune system

- Reduces toxin accumulation

For the Mind & Emotions:

- Treats insomnia and anxiety

- Alleviates nervous tension evoked by bad news

- Calms a hyperactive mind

- Helps people handle sorrow and frustration

Now that you have learned the body & mind benefits that different oils offer, and you know how to blend the oils and keep the general precautions in mind, you can use your imagination and intuition and make your own blends. Enjoy!

Chapter 6 Health Spa: Body & Mind Detox Weekend Program

If you think that this chapter is about some highly restrictive detox diet based only on juicing, have no fear: it's not. The approach that I decided to apply here is based on some general guidelines to get you introduced to a healthy, balanced alkaline diet based on organic products, including plenty of fresh fruits and vegetables and integral cereals.

I am not saying that I am not fan of juicing and other cleansing programs. I love them, but these programs can be too restrictive for some people, especially if you are doing the cleanse on your own. Moreover, before starting on of the above-mentioned cleansing program, especially if it is restricted to juicing, it is advisable to contact a specialist or a naturopathy doctor so that they can design a program especially for you.

The purpose of this chapter is to make you feel energized when you wake up on Monday: a weekend daily Spa at home with your aromatherapy treatments and holistic relaxation should be accompanied by a natural diet so that you can rejuvenate. Feel free to create your own program based on the guidelines and suggestions included. I hope that you will fall in love with healthy living and make it a part of your lifestyle. If you are pregnant, lactating, anaemic, have any serious medical conditions, or are on medication, don't get started on this program until you have consulted with a medical doctor.

Preparations:

- To create your daily health spa at home, make sure that you choose a weekend or some other dates when you are not working and won't be disturbed

- Plan lots of time for relaxation as well as sleep. Some people see sleeping as a waste of time because our Western world and mentality have programmed us for active-living and the pursuit of success. As much as I love working on my goals, I also make sure that I create my health home spa regularly and just relax.

If you have a car, you probably take care of it by getting it fixed and maintained regularly. Especially if you drive a nice car, you want it to last longer and remain in the same condition it was in when you bought it. The same is true with your body, which is far more important than your car!

Jim Rohn said: *Take care of your body, that's the only place you have to live.*

Many life coaches and success coaches emphasize the importance of maintaining excellent health. Most of them prioritize it before financial or social success. Without good health one cannot travel, pursue a career, or enjoy a great relationship. Restore health and balance with a regular home spa ritual. Get ready with a few before-you-get-started tips:

- As much as you can, switch off your mobile, PC, and TV, and avoid Facebook, Twitter and other social media. Make sure that you get equipped with some good reads. Just choose whatever you like to read to totally disconnect your mind. An aromatherapy bath accompanied by a good book has many body & mind benefits. It will help you relax and slow down.

- If you have roommates or live with your family, let them know what you're planning to do and invite them, too.

- Plan some activities like walking. (If you can get out of the city to soothe your mind, your body will get energized immediately.)

- Prepare some relaxation music or some kind of music that puts you in a good mood.

- Before starting your weekend health spa, make sure that you go shopping for organic food. Fill your refrigerator and kitchen cupboards with fresh fruits and vegetables, integral cereals like millet, algae, amaranth, cuscus, nuts, legumes and herbal infusions.

The following suggestions will help you to wake up refreshed on Monday morning and experience some body & mind rejuvenation:

- Eliminate coffee, black tea and alcohol since they can only aggravate stress and emotional tension. Replace them with green tea (in moderate amounts because it contains theine as well), fresh vegetable juices, and plenty of clean water. - Eliminate processed foods, along with sugar (sweets like cakes, biscuits, artificial honey and chocolate). Choose healthy snacks instead, like bananas, nuts and dried fruits.

- Eliminate - or at least reduce - dairy products and replace cow's milk with vegan milk, such as rice milk, or almond milk or coconut milk(all great for vegan smoothies).

More Health Spa Tips:

- Instead of frying vegetables, steam them.

- Eat fruits between the meals as snacks. Eating fruits after a meal can cause indigestion, which in turn results in lack of energy.

- To avoid unhealthy food cravings, prepare yourself: plan four to five daily meals. For example, try juicing for breakfast, healthy, gluten-free grains lime quinoa + veggies/salad for lunch, a smoothie in the afternoon and a light dinner based on steamed vegetables or a soup. Feel free to adapt your ideas to your own food preferences, climate zone and season.

I have a free eBook you can download at:

www.HolisticWellnessProject.com/alkaline

- Include herbal teas, such as: white tea, roibosh tea, tea of three years, or, if you wish to relax, try chamomile, valerian, Californian Poppy or passion flower.

- Do not force yourself into eating foods that you don't like. There are many healthy foods that you can choose, so adapt your diet to your personal preferences and lifestyle.

- Include green vegetables and juice them too. Experiment with new juices to fuel your body & mind.

- Make sure that your diet is rich in antioxidant foods, such as broccoli, carrots, oranges, lemons, strawberries, and blueberries. As a general guideline, try to choose the fruits and vegetables that are grown in your climate zone as much as you can. Each climate zone is abundant in certain foods, and many macrobiotic food experts are starting to point out the importance of preferring foods grown in your climate zone rather than from far away countries. For example, if you live in Northern Europe, Canada, or the Northern USA, you may go for carrots rather than oranges or some tropical foods; however if you live in New Zealand or Australia, you should definitely take advantage of kiwis.

- If you are allergic to or intolerant of any of the foods mentioned here, or suspect some intolerances, avoid them and consult with a naturopathy doctor for a personalized solutions.

The benefits that you get by making the above-mentioned adjustments as much as you can (again, don't be harsh on yourself and build up slowly instead) will make you feel more vitalized and focused as you will get rid of toxins and start taking better care of your internal organs.

BONUS CHAPTER:

Discover All Your Senses and Feel Rejuvenated in Just a Few Seconds

Have you ever wondered where our feelings of anxiety and depressions are coming from? Most of the time, these feelings are not actually about ourselves, but rather about the things that are NOT happening to us at the present moment. There are times when we find ourselves nostalgically drifting towards the past, longing for things to go back to the way they used to be.

There are also moments when we find ourselves fussing and worrying over what would happen in the future. We are everywhere, but here. We say that the grass is always greener on the other side of the fence, or somewhere else, but not where we actually are. We are waiting for the unexpected to happen. We have traveled back in time and into the future, but have never managed to remain in the present moment. We have become restless souls, always searching, always looking, and never standing still.

How then, do we break away from this fatal cycle of restlessness? The answer is quite simple, my friend. Meditate.

Be aware that you are here, now, and find peace in the process. This does not mean that you have to sit still or look very calm physically. Personally, I have met many people who seemed to be really focused and calm from the outside, but they would admit that deep inside they were lost and torn. At the same time, I have met people who seemed active, always moving around and sometimes expressing their anger straight away, but deep inside they had their peace of mind. As they say - *don't judge the book by the cover.*

Be present. This is the core message of the practice of meditation. It seems like an easy task, but can be quite challenging to achieve. Let me challenge you now. Put this book down, close your eyes and allow yourself to be the king (or queen) of your castle. Breathe in and out the way you feel is right for you. Keep telling your subconscious mind, "I am in control. I control how I feel. My emotions work for me." It's up to you how much time you decide to devote to this process. I always find it really energizing and uplifting, and just like yoga stretches that allow me to move and feel my body, this meditation reminds me that I create my own feelings. I like to repeat this process a few times a day (just like yoga poses). Short sessions, but repeated throughout the day, do wonders for my well-being and they help me develop new, empowering habits. Besides, I never get bored when going through this process and I never stress out thinking I don't have time.

You don't even have two minutes for the most important meeting today? The meeting with yourself? Then, how come you can be prepared for other meetings with your bosses, colleagues, employees, clients, family and friends..? If you want to be changing the world and maybe impress/help other people, you must first impress/help yourself. In order to achieve it, you must become a master of self-care. The master of self-care!

Mindfulness is the heart of the practice of meditation. This is the act of consciously bringing your awareness to the present moment without judgment and attachment. When you are mindful, you are going through each moment with a heightened awareness of your surroundings, thoughts, feelings and bodily sensations. Using your five senses, together with your breath, to bring awareness to the present moment, is one of the easiest ways to achieve a mindful state. There are no mantras to chant or difficult postures to perform. Of course, you can always explore them later, down the road. Meditation is a life-long study.

Meditating using your five senses it the most literal way to direct your consciousness to the present moment. It can effortlessly bring you to a relaxed state. Once you find yourself in a relaxed state, you can gently and easily quiet your mind. A quiet and still mind allows you listen to the callings of your heart, soul and the Universe. It can propel you to a higher level of consciousness and awareness that is shared with the Divine.

Discover all your senses by going through this simple and easy guided meditation:

Let us begin by finding a comfortable seating position. You can sit on a half or full lotus position, if you are familiar with the pose, or you can simply cross your legs. We are not looking for a perfect asana or posture here. What matters is that you are comfortable.

Lift the crown of your head towards the heavens while grounding your sit bone to the earth. Feel your spine lengthening. Your neck is soft and long. Feel proud of yourself, you are taking one of the most important steps on your spiritual journey. You are discovering yourself. Feeling, looking and being proud is not wrong, you deserve it.

Find openness in your chest. Feel your lungs expanding. Feel the rush of the air going through your nostrils. Breathe in through the nose and exhale through your nose. Find a rhythm as you feel the air going in and out of your body. Let it caress you like gentle waves in the ocean rocking you gently. Simply observe without judgment how your breath goes back and forth until you feel your muscles begin to relax. Unclench your jaw. It's unbelievable how much tension can accumulate there and in your throat chakra. Relax your face and your eyelids. Relax the soles of your feet. Let you body find rest in the gentle lull of your breath. Squeeze your eyebrows a few times to get rid of tension; it's like a gentle self-massage. Using all your fingers, massage your forehead - again, we tend to accumulate way too much tension than we can handle.

Now that you are relaxed, we will begin our journey to discover your senses. You are safe here. This is where you belong. Rest assured that your body is protected. You can let go. Allow your mind and soul to travel and flow freely.

See. You are on a beach. You are standing on the shore and gently gazing out to the horizon. You don't need to stare and strain your eyes. Simply let your gaze fall gently towards the horizon of the ocean. Be aware of its vastness and the distance spanned by the horizon. Notice the enormity of the ocean right before you. Don't feel overwhelmed, don't be afraid. Enjoy it and relax in it.

Slowly, dip into the waters and begin to float towards the horizon. Don't chase it relentlessly. Simply allow yourself to lightly float towards it. There is no pressure to reach it. You are simply unhurriedly, gently and quietly moving towards the horizon.

Hear. As you effortlessly float towards the horizon, you bring your awareness to the sound of water sloshing around you as you continue to float towards the horizon. You then become aware of the sound of the waves gently crashing into the shore. You can hear the bubbles fizzle as the waves break. You can hear the waters receding back into the vastness of the ocean. You listen to waves once again lapping on the shore. It goes back and forth, and slowly, you find yourself falling into its unique rhythm. It becomes your lullaby as the waves gently rock you to a peaceful slumber.

Feel. You were about to fall asleep when you suddenly find yourself washed ashore. You feel the wet sand on your face. You feel it's grittiness on your palms as you push yourself up and turn your body over. Finally, you are now lying on your back. You can still feel the wet and cold sand underneath you, but this time, you are also savoring the warmth of the sun as it gently shines down on you. You allow the sun to bathe you in its warmth. You feel your clothes slowly drying up.

As the sun continues to shine down on you, you decide to get up and walk towards the island. You are barefoot, but you don't mind. You like the feel of the find sand on your feet and on your toes. They tickle you a little bit, but you're okay with that. Sand walking massages your feet in an all natural way. You feel like you're at the most luxurious SPA there is!

Be aware of how solid the ground is beneath you, even when you feel your feet leaving footprints on the sand. Be conscious of the feeling of stability that the earth brings you and continue walking.

Smell. As you keep on walking, you become aware of a sweet, fragrant smell coming from the woods that stand right before you.

You decided to follow the sweet scent and you make your way through the thicket and undergrowth, until you find yourself in a clearing. In the middle, is a small patch of rose bushes. The flowers are in full bloom and you find yourself filling your lungs with their sweet smelling scent.

The fragrance of the roses fills your soul with renewed vigor. You feel rejuvenated and invigorated after swimming for so long in the ocean.

You go from one flower to another, gently smelling them. You are in no rush because you know that you can always go back to them. The roses are like a gift of life. They renew your spirit and ask for nothing in return.

Taste. While you continue to explore the small garden you found in the middle of the clearing, you begin to feel hunger from swimming and walking for so long. Your hunger pulls you away from the roses and towards the small cottage at the edge of the clearing. You are able to allow yourself to easily leave the roses behind because you know that their sweet fragrance will last forever in your soul. You will never forget them. Your soul will always remind you of their sweet and aromatic smell whenever you need to rejuvenate.

You walk towards the cabin until you reach the front door. You slowly open the door and you are greeted by the most delectable aroma of food. There is soup boiling on the stove on the far corner of the cabin. The long table in the middle is laden with different kinds of healing foods. Before you is a feast fit for a king and queen...

You slowly make your way towards the table. You sit and start eating. You are mindful of each bite you take. You enjoy eating tropical fruits and other natural treats from Mother Earth. You see to it that you are eating slowly, enjoying and savoring each scrumptious meal. You are careful not to stuff your mouth with different kinds of food all at the same time. You allow yourself to take one bite at a time. You chew the food thoroughly until it begins to melt in your mouth. You take pleasure in every bite you take. The next bite is always more scrumptious than the last one. You do this with the other food on the table, until you find yourself full and sated.

After your meal, you look around you and see the bedroom. You walk towards it and gently open the door. Inside is a huge bed with soft pillows and warm blankets. You lie on it and rest.

You are nourished, rejuvenated, warm and safe. You let your head fall gently on the pillow made of feathers and, slowly, you close your eyes.

Your journey has ended. You rest your body, knowing tomorrow will be another adventure. You will receive new gifts, you will witness new sights, you will taste more delectable food, you will gain new experiences and life will be much richer. But for now, you rest and allow yourself to relish in the triumphs of today...

Conclusion

I hope this book was able to titillate your imagination and inspire you to create your own home **wellness and health spa**. You can now apply the techniques that I have shared with you or simply use them as guidelines to create your own. I also encourage you to relax holistically with your family and friends. Invite them to come around and enjoy all the amazing spa treatments based on aromatherapy, gentle massages, facial treatments, relaxation, music therapy and body & mind fuelling foods. I hope that you will realize the many benefits of creating your own spa at home and start experimenting to find the treatments that will best work to improve your body, mind, as soul.

- Creating your home spa is an affordable way to relax at home.

- You can adjust and personalize your treatments.

- You can inspire your loved ones and help them relax, too.

- You can develop a series of your own holistic beauty treatments.

- You will take control of how you feel and learn to cope with stress effectively and in a fun way.

You should definitely give it a try and treat yourself to some pleasurable and luxurious SPA treatments in the comfort of your own home!

One more thing...I might need your help!

If you enjoyed this book and received value from it, could you please share your experience with other readers? One sentence review on Amazon is enough, and it will surely make my day and encourage me to create more books (and very soon - courses) for you!

If there is something you don't understand, have questions, suggestions, and/or doubts, **please** e-mail me at:

info@holisticwellnessproject.com

I am here to help.

You can also find me at:

www.facebook.com/HolisticWellnessProject

www.instagram.com/Marta_Wellness

Remember to join my newsletter so that we can keep in touch!

I will also guide you with tons of motivational and inspirational messages that will help you keep on track and embrace wellness the way you deserve.

www.holisticwellnessproject.com

Free Wellness Newsletter

Before you go, I would love to offer you a free copy of my book: "Revolutionize Your Life with Alkaline Foods" + free access to my wellness newsletter.

It will help you achieve total wellbeing through healing alkaline foods and drinks! Healing from the inside out- aromatherapy and Alkalinity go hand in hand!

Free Sign Up Link:

www.holisticwellnessproject.com/alkaline

ABOUT MARTA TUCHOWSKA

Marta Tuchowska is a passionate holistic wellness coach and author on a mission. She wants to help you create a healthy body, mind and spirit through a balanced lifestyle. Marta has a strong background in healing and health (certified in massage therapy, holistic nutrition, aromatherapy and Reiki), and she infuses her natural therapy knowledge with motivational and life coaching to help you create a life full of energy, health and happiness. Marta wants to make it easy, doable and fun. She calls it holistic lifestyle design for modern, 21st-century, busy folks! Join the exciting journey of total body and mind transformation at: www.HolisticWellnessProject.com.

CPSIA information can be obtained
at www.ICGtesting.com
Printed in the USA
BVHW020731140220
572304BV00021B/1097

9 781913 575144